PERENNIAL QUESTIONS

Original title in German :

EWIGE FRAGEN

Die religösen Grundprobleme und ihre Lösung
im Indischen Geiste.

PERENNIAL QUESTIONS

The Fundamental Religious Problems and their Solution in Indian Thought

An Introduction to the Philosophical Religions

GEORGE GRIMM

Translated from the German by

Ch. PÖNISCH-SCHOENWERTH

Edited by

M. KELLER-GRIMM and M. HOPPE

MOTILAL BANARSIDASS

Delhi :: Varanasi :: Patna

Indological Publishers & Booksellers
Head Office : Bungalow Road, Jawahar Nagar, Delhi-7
Branches : 1. Chowk, Varanasi-1 (U.P.)
2. Ashok Rajpath, Patna-4 (Bihar)

First Edition : *Delhi*, 1979

Printed in India
By Shantilal Jain, at Shri Jainendra Press,
A-45, Phase-I, Industrial Area, Naraina, New Delhi-110 028,
Published by Narendra Prakash Jain, for Motilal Banarsidass,
Bungalow Road, Jawahar Nagar, Delhi-110 007.

FOREWORD

Whence have I come from and where shall I go to? What does the imperishable happiness I long for consist in, and where is it to be found? Do these questions not present themselves very likely to everybody at least once, in an hour of inner stillness, and do they not change such an hour into an hour of deep thoughtfulness! They actually are "perennial questions"; as such they arise ever anew with the vicissitudes of life, both in the East and in the West.

In German-speaking countries *Perennial Questions* has pointed out to its readers in how excelling a way the early Indian thought answered the religious questions in their profundity. The primary longing keeps alive within us the very longing for accomplishment and harmony. It is bodhi-citta, the divine spark, the awakening-impulse latent in every being. Thus we experience the condition of permanent dissatisfaction and constant desiring as a state that is inadequate and contrary to our true Being. This primary longing within us demands detachment from what has become and is conditioned as well as turning ourselves towards the non-conditioned.

The answers the following expositions give to the reader's questions come from intuitive knowledge, to which in the Occident both the great Plotinos and Meister Eckhart have also penetrated. Here the writer of this foreword thinks of S. Radhakrishnan, who stated that while the different religions, as concerns their historical manifestations, join us together into strictly delimited groups and oppose a loyal attitude towards world-wide solidarity, the true mystics have at all times stood up for human friendliness. They are beyond the competition of creeds and likewise beyond racial conflicts and national quarrels. As a spiritual religion true mysticism eludes *both the extremes of dogmatic statements and of dogmatic negation.* To all appearances it is called to be the very religion for the future.

To the contents of these expositions of S. Radhakrishnan, whose writings strongly impress many deeper minds in the Occident, I add the following expositions of the German philosopher Arthur Schopenhauer, who largely paved the way for the Indian thought in the western world: "Nothing can be more astonishing than the harmony with each other among the writers who expound those teachings, notwithstanding the immense difference as to their epoch, country and religion, together with the unshakable certainty and fervent trust with which they make known their inner experience as a whole. They actually do not constitute a *sect* that sticks to, defends and passes on a once adopted and theoretically convenient dogma; they rather do not, for the most part, know of each other; yea, the Indian, Christian and Mohammedan mystics, quietists and ascetics are heterogeneous in everything except in the intrinsic meaning and spirit of their teachings."

In India the conclusion of the Vedas was brought by the Upanishads in the Vedanta, which implied the ultimate goal of Deliverance and stated that harmony and peace are to be found but in one's own innermost, to which the psycho-technical way was shown by Yoga. This spiritual trend attained to its highest perfection in the Teaching of the Buddha, the Wholly Awakened One. It is He who gives the clearest answer, an answer again and again approached by the religious genius and which has been given expression to anew in more recent times by Sri Ramana Maharishi, the Saint from Tiruvannamalai in South India: "The birth of the I-thought is the person's birth, and the former's death is the death of the latter, too. After the I-thought has arisen it comes to the false identification with the body. But once you have ceased to identify yourself with the body and the real Self has become reality, that delusion vanishes."

Therewith the true seeker is given an answer to the "perennial questions", in that he more and more attains to the very certainty that all that which is transient and perishable about and around him, and which brings him suffering ever anew in the measure of his attachment, has but the nature of an attribute and ultimately cannot touch his true Self. From this very certainty he draws a world-overcoming force, a force that is utterly necessary in particular in the present time's everyday life to enable him to remain mindful despite the sense-impressions showering down upon him. Here the gem within the Lotus shows itself, the very treasure within one's own innermost, a treasure which the world cannot give, but which it cannot take away either.

The editors are greatly indebted to Mrs. Ch. Pönisch-Schoenwerth for having done the translation to which her inner relationship to the book's contents particularly enabled her.

Utting Max Hoppe
January, 1979

A

I

All life, all existence has but one sole purpose, namely to lead to happiness, to make happy. "*We are beings who crave for happiness and detest suffering*", declares the Buddha. On account of this the beings continually ponder over how they could become happy, and when they fancy to have become so they worry and trouble themselves about remaining happy. All concern and effort in business and profession, in handicrafts and arts, science and technology, trade and politics aim but at making happy oneself and maybe also others. All statesmen and economists, the greater they are, the more they aim at making the people happy. All philosophers search for imperishable happiness, all religions promise their believers everlasting bliss. The yearning for happiness is so deeply rooted in man that no power in the world ever shall turn him from it. Even he who out of despair puts an end to his life does so only in the hope thus to find rest and peace and therewith happiness, or to become in any case happier than he is at present.

II

Now what must there be for man to become happy? A simple lady of the world once answered this question to the point; on being asked what kind of eternal happiness she hoped to experience after death she promptly replied : "All I want is peace and quiet". In fact, these words comprise the unmistakable criterion of real, true happiness, since as long as restlessness, anxiety and disquietude still prevail in man, so long is he not happy but, on the very contrary, unhappy; instead of being happy, he suffers. For, it is quite a matter of course to everybody that as long as one is tormented with inner restlessness one suffers. It is because of this that the Buddha says : "*Where there is no inner peace, there is suffering*".

Now when is there no inward peace, and when does thus restlessness prevail ? When there is an unfulfilled desire within us, since every unsatisfied desire torments us. It is on account of this that all men, yea all beings upon the whole incessantly try to satisfy their wishes in order to be released from the inward torment, from the inward restlessness called forth by those unfulfilled desires; indeed, they do seek to realise them with a greediness not even shrinking back from violence and murder.

But why do men have so many desires ? Because their present condition and the circumstances they are at present compelled to live in are not adequate to them, hence because they are not appropriate to their innermost Being. They lack something, they still miss something in order to become happy; in fact, they still lack a great deal, they still miss a great deal for their present position really to suit them, namely so that they could state : "My present state is perfectly suitable to me, perfectly adequate; I am now absolutely content and therewith actually happy !" However, here on earth the beings are so far from this state that Meister Eckhart exclaimed, "All beings inwardly bear bitterness."

From this it is clear that if the beings were in a state *perfectly* adequate to them they would no longer will or desire anything. Indeed, one can desire but what one lacks. In a state perfectly adequate to us we should, consequently, no longer lack anything and therewith no longer desire anything either. For, where there still is a lack of something, the state is not, for this very reason, a *perfectly* adequate one. Thus in a state perfectly adequate to us no desire at all ever could dwell within us any more. Yea, if we were to ask a being which is in a state absolutely adequate to it what it furthermore desires and wishes, it would answer : "To desire ? To wish ? What kind of a thing is that ? Is it red, or blue, or black ?"—

But if no wish at all arises within us, then there no longer is any inward restlessness, any inward disharmony either. For, all inward restlessness and disharmony is but a restlessness of *will*, a disharmony of *will : "All the tempests' uproar derives solely from one's own will, whether one realises it or not"*, says Meister Eckhart. Thus, if we were in a state absolutely adequate to us we should not only be wholly desireless but there would also reside perfect inward peace within us. "He who has quenched all his will and all his wish, he has peace" (Meister Eckhart).

Let us summarise the above expositions :

For man really to be perfectly happy he must be in a state *perfectly* and *absolutely* adequate to him. But if he were in a state absolutely adequate to him he would, consequently, no longer have any desire, he would be, hence, perfectly desireless, perfectly happy. Were he, however, desirelessly happy, then all inner disharmony—which, as previously stated, derives but from unsatisfied desiring—would be put an end to; therewith boundless peace, the *Great Peace* would dwell within him. Consequently, perfect happiness, perfectly adequate state, perfect desirelessness and perfect inner peace are identical concepts; at bottom all these words state the selfsame thing. Conversely it follows that where there is a desire, a will, there is an inadequate state, the conquest of which is our will's sole purpose. As this conquest won't succeed and the will is, on the contrary, continuously frustrated, beings find themselves at the mercy of inner disharmony and therewith of suffering. All willing and hence all suffering are therefore merely the symptoms of an inadequate situation and disappear with the latter : in an absolutely adequate state not even the trace of a willing or suffering is possible.

III

Naturally, here the very question arises : is it actually possible for the beings to attain such a state perfectly and absolutely adequate to them, a state in which to all eternity no further desire can arise, in particular not even the desire for the state attained to change, for another state to take its place ? Is there, hence, actually a perfect, absolute happiness which beings can attain ? Here we are conscious of having arrived at the primary problem of all existence. But is it actually possible for this primary problem to be solved ? However surprising it may appear, it is even quite easy to solve : the desire for an absolutely adequate state is the primary longing of every human heart, yea of all beings upon the whole. As long as they have not yet attained this state of absolute happiness they are not wholly satisfied, and so long, consequently, do they not find any rest, any peace, but must go on struggling and striving towards that state. Only when a being can declare of itself : "Now I am *perfectly* well", all desiring and therewith all striving and struggling shall come to an end.

Thus the absolutely adequate state actually is the deepest and ultimate desire, the primary longing of all beings. But for a primary longing common to all beings realisation must certainly be possible. For indeed, nature always and infallibly achieves its deepest and ultimate purposes, though only after immeasurable periods of time. Nature acts in the line of least resistance; accordingly, it does not, in particular, produce any needs for which there is no help. All the more must then be possible the satisfaction of the deepest need, namely of the primary longing for an *absolutely* adequate state : beings would not have this primary longing at all if it were not capable of realisation. If *we* have not yet discovered the path leading towards this ultimate and ideal state it is due but to our own weakness, our own wretchedness, not to objective reality.

This can also be made clear thus : the longing for an absolutely adequate state is the *primary impulse* of all beings; it springs forth from the deepest recesses of Reality, from the lightless realm of the primordial source, which is no longer illuminated by any cognition and in which whatever exists has its roots, and wherein for this very reason the purpose of all that which exists is likewise comprised. Therewith this primary impulse at the same time shows itself to be the non-delusive and thereby absolutely unequivocal herald of the beings' ultimate destination. As such it shall not rest before its goal, the absolutely adequate state, is achieved, even though this should take world-periods. It is the whip that again and again, unceasingly and untiringly goads the beings on in this direction. Hence it follows that if the primary impulse of a being comes to extinction and it therewith attains peace, this is the manifestation of its having achieved the absolutely adequate state. Thus it has fulfilled its destination, as Lao Tse expressly says in the following words : "To come to rest means to have fulfilled one's destination".

Lao Tse, however, goes on saying: "To have fulfilled one's destination means to be in harmony with the eternal order, and to be in harmony with the eternal order means to be Accomplished." These words are now easily comprehended: the eternal order is precisely that one in which every being dwells in the state absolutely adequate to it. Only such an order is unchangeable, i.e. eternal. As long and in so far as this order is perturbed, disorder sets in. During this disturbance the eternal order strives after the elimination of this upset, and it does so precisely in the primary impulse that is to reinstall us in the eternal order: it objects, grieves and threatens as bad conscience after every deed in contradiction with it, and it makes us happy in a good conscience after every act in harmony with the state absolutely adequate to beings. Only when a being has achieved this state, the herald of the eternal order, the primary impulse, is, as stated above, silenced, and is so for ever : such an "Accomplished One" is no longer moved and urged at all from within — boundless peace, the Great Peace abides in him. Indeed, he has "done what was to be done", since he has fulfilled his destination. Consequently, a state absolutely adequate to us is immediately comprised in the eternal order, wherewith its realization is not only possible, but is in truth the essential task of our life.--Kant has given expression to this in a few words : "You can, for you ought".

IV

Naturally, this much is certain: here on earth this state absolutely adequate to us cannot be realised; apart from everything else, on earth there rules death as a natural law admitting of no exception, a law that demonstrates that all beings are doomed to die, also the human ones, at present and in the future. Yet in a state perfectly and absolutely adequate to us there could, of course, no longer be any dying for us. For, how could it ever be possible for us to experience as *perfectly* adequate a state in which we should have to admit at every instant : "Though I now feel perfectly happy, in no time the whole splendour shall come to an end, for I must die!" It is on this account that a German poet exclaims: "Ah, what makes us happy ought to be permanent !"

Thus we have found that a state absolutely adequate to us actually must be possible; this is vouched for by the deep longing we bear within us for that state, yea it is vouched for by the eternal world-order itself. In this absolutely adequate state there ought to be no death and dying for us any longer; otherwise the state would not be absolutely adequate to us. While on earth this state is utterly impossible, since there rules death as a natural law allowing of no exception. Consequently, the state absolutely adequate to us must have its realm beyond this earth, hence in another world. Therefore, he who wants to dwell in the absolutely adequate state permanently must emigrate to that other world. However, we can only emigrate to another world when we put aside our present body which due to all the conditions of life inevitably ties us to this earth; consequently we can do so only in our death.

Therewith two entirely new problems present themselves, namely the problem of our immortality and the problem whether there actually is a beyond to which we can emigrate. Yet even both these problems are already decided for him to whom the preceding expositions are clear : if it is true that our primary longing for a state perfectly adequate to us cannot be delusive, and if it is true that on earth the realization of this state is impossible — (both these points are, as we have seen, obvious) — then, for this very reason, it is equally true that we are not reduced to naught by death, and that there must be a beyond in which the state absolutely adequate to us can be realised.

In which high degree all this is obvious to the great majority of men already follows from the fact that nothing can divert them from their faith in the non-delusive nature of their *primary feeling*, their *primary instinct*, not even the evident impossibility of really becoming permanently happy here on earth, nor any proof by an alleged science that man be annihilated in death. With an invisible hammer this *primary feeling*, this *primary instinct* again and again, at every instant hammers into the hearts of men: "Your longing for a perfect and hence deathless state of happiness must in any case be capable of realization, and as it can by no means come true while here on earth, its realization necessarily must be possible in the beyond." — Guided by this primary feeling, by this primary instinct, man regardlessly puts his trust in religions, which proclaim the perfectly happy state in a heavenly world; he trusts in them even though they cannot demonstrate to him his immortality nor this heavenly realm either but, on the very contrary, demand belief. This belief is not difficult for him, just because it has its unshakable mainstay in the primary longing and feeling of man himself. Therein lies the indestructible power of all religions that proclaim a beyond.

V

Belief is not, however, the highest form of cognition, since it consists but in our faith in the certainty of another man's assertion. Certainty, however, is achieved only by one's own insight into the correctness of an assertion, by the rational proof of its correctness; indeed, perfect certainty is brought about only by *intuitive* cognition, hence by oneself *experiencing* a fact. Thus from time immemorial all men who could not content themselves with the mere primary feeling of their immortality—(as Spinoza says, "we feel and experience that we are immortal") — and with the mere feeling of the existence of higher worlds sought to convey these felt truths into clear cognition. They sought to prove them according to the rules of reason, yea they strived after personally experiencing while here on earth their immortality and the existence of a heavenly realm in which the state perfectly adequate to us comes true.

It is evident that only the morally and intellectually most outstanding *geniuses* of mankind were capable of such an undertaking. Sublime flashes of light pointing to this direction shine towards us from Greek philosophy, above all from the profound wisdom of the great Neo-Platonist Plotinos, then from the Christian mystics of whom Meister Eckhart has reached dizzy heights, a wisdom that Angelus Silesius succeeded in popularizing in his incomparable pithy sayings.

Above all the ancient Āryan Indians were fascinated by the idea of a cognitive solution of the primary problems of religion; thus it is no wonder that they finally succeeded in finding their definitive solution. The reader has a right to this statement being proved to him.

The religious wisdom of the ancient Āryan Indians is collected in the Vedas; likewise that of Christianity is treasured in the Bible, only the Veda is by far more voluminous than the latter. Veda means "knowledge", namely the religious, the sacred knowledge as revealed by wise seers, by rishis. The earliest part of the Vedas is the Rigveda, which goes back to 2600-2500 B.C. and, according to some scholars, even to earlier times. The most recent part of the Vedas are the Upanishads, which were completed about 500 B.C.

At bottom it was also the ancient Āryan Indian's main concern to fathom his actual relationship to the world he saw himself placed in; therewith also he aimed at inquiring into the future awaiting man after death. Also to him—as to all men upon the whole—it was quite self-evident that the question of whither we shall go can only be solved successfully if it is at first ascertained whence we do come, i.e. where everything, yea this whole phenomenal world which we have to fight our way through does come from or, as Schopenhauer says, "Who am I? What is this world which has come upon me like a dream of whose beginning I am not aware?"[1]

Thus also the ancient Āryan Indian regarded the problem of the *world-bottom* as the essence of his quest for religious cognition. Everybody, be he the simplest man, from day gone by feels that the phenomenal world cannot have its sufficient motivation within itself, since no cognizable cause is the sufficient cause for its effect. Thus the coming into existence of the higher developed living beings is conditioned by there being a male and a female germ-cell and by their uniting into one. These material alterations are the cause of a new living being of like species as its parents as result. But it is wholly incomprehensible how it is possible for these previously mentioned processes, which result in generation, to supply the very condition for the

1. Trsl. by E.F.J. Payne.

most ingenious of productions, the basis of the indescribably complicated human organism, whose infinite complexity and perfection only he knows who has studied anatomy, as Schopenhauer says. Consequently, there must be something that endows the fecunded germ-cell with its particular causative nature which enables it to produce a living being constructed with incomparable ingenuity, a being whose sensations and mental activities later on may rise to the heights of the genius that withdraws the veil from the world. Naturally, the same applies to the animal organisms which in all essential aspects do not differ from the human ones. Thus, to give only one example out of many, the homogeneous, shapeless liquid of the bird-egg assumes the so complex and exactly defined shape proper to the genus and species of a bird as soon as the appropriate temperature supervenes. Is the supervening warmth supposed to be the sufficient reason for this to happen? But alone, by itself, this warmth could at most make the liquid of the bird's egg become warmer, and nothing else.— Apart from this in the animal world there also is the miracle of the artistic impulses and of mimicry; those living beings endowed with them do strive with utter resoluteness after aims they certainly have no idea of, and they do so with such perfection that he who is conversant with the matter is lost in awe-struck amazement at the mysterious force here in operation.— Where do the miracles of the plants' world have their roots ? There rule, exactly as in the human and animal realms and defying any physical explanations, the vital and healing-powers as well as instinct and urge for beauty, i.e. all that which we call the soul's activity.— Which is the reason for the seed of the quassia to turn all sap it draws from the earth into bitterness, and for the sugar-cane's seed to turn it into sweetness? Are the material components of the seed taken up by the earth the cause or the earth itself? Everybody feels that such an assertion would be a folly.—Which is the sufficient reason for the sap of even the tallest and mightiest trees to rise, in defiance of gravity, to the highest and smallest branches and twigs at the tree's top?—Wherein do the energies effective in minerals root? What makes a match burst into flames when rubbed on the rough surface of the match-box? As yet no chemist has found the fire either in the match or in the striking surface, and it won't ever be discovered therein.—

What does — to cast our eyes beyond our earth —ultimately underlie the countless worlds that present themselves to us as the nocturnal starry sky, worlds of which many glide along as fixed stars with their planets at so remote distances from the earth that for their light to reach us a period of millions of years is reckoned to be necessary, though this light covers 300,000 kilometres a second?—

What underlies the laws according to which these innumerable worlds rotate within space in such perfect harmony that none of them collides with the others despite the orbit partly being so very complex — (which is, e.g., the case with the double stars' planets and with several suns)—that, after Littrow, the mathematical analysis with all its perfection is not in a position to determine even in the rough those extremely complicated movements!—

What does actually underlie the laws that rule the universe ? Though these laws disappear with the destruction of the forms in which they operate they immediately break forth anew when the conditions therefor required are given afresh, even though it be after billions of years, from which it follows that these laws themselves are never at all destroyed but merely become invisible.—

The perfect insufficiency of every cognizable physical cause for its effect and the resultant necessity of assuming a hidden factor in the course of the world — (a factor with the knowledge of which everything would be so thoroughly elucidated that no riddles and doubts would be left over) —, these two points have hitherto pressed themselves overwhelmingly upon every thinking man's mind. *They* are the actual and deepest motivation of all belief in God, yea its unshakable basis for all times.

Taken in this sense the God-concept is a *necessary* product of all thinking in accordance with the rules of reason. Yea, in this respect we cannot speak of a belief, but rather of a knowledge of God. This is why the God-consciousness is ineradicably established in man and why the latter cannot definitively content himself with a philosophical system that does not bring forth this God-consciousness as its very bloom.

Therewith we have at the same time penetrated to the essence of the God-concept: there is a hidden and mysterious factor in the events of the world,[2] a factor that alone endows the only cognizable causes, namely the occasional ones, with their

2. God=the Ātman in beings.

causality, i.e. their nature causative of such inconceivable, marvellous effects; yea, it is this hidden factor that the events of the world derive their substance from and that even their mere possibility is comprised in. It is precisely the designation of this mysterious, marvellous factor that the name 'God' —(which comprehends all that which is mysterious and marvellous)—is intended for; thence it becomes at the same time clear that the name 'God' is but another expression for the world's bottom.

It is evident that in this world-bottom also lies the solution of the primary problems we have so far worked out, namely the problem of the state absolutely adequate to us, then that of immortality and finally the problem of a beyond after death; hence it follows that the solution of these problems actually can be only derived from *it*. Thus at all times and everywhere men have searched and do search for the world-bottom, and they do search for it through cognition in their philosophies, and in so far as this cognition does not suffice men search for the bottom of the world through belief in their religions, the latter's expression for the world-bottom being God, the Godhead, the Divine.

VI

Commonly men do try to approach the Divine in the above sense through all possible investigation of the external world and its laws. This, however, is a complete nonsense. Because, as has been already stated, God is the world's *bottom*. Yet the *bottom* of the world does not lie on the outside, on the world's surface; as the ultimate ground, as the basis of the entire phenomenal world, it is only to be found at the very bottom, yea at the deepest bottom of the world. Thus it is just as impossible to illuminate this bottom through outer investigation as it is, for instance, to elucidate the bottom of the ocean by examining the waters that cover it. This clearly shows the silliness of the words of an astronomer of the past century who affirmed that he had explored the whole firmament with his telescope without having found God. Since natural science concerns itself merely with the *phenomena* of nature it cannot even conceptually ever penetrate to the world's bottom, from which the whole of nature springs forth, a fact confirmed already by the well-known physicist Du Bois-Reymond in the significant words, "ignoramus et ignorabimus : we do not know it, and we never shall experience it either". It was in particular Goethe who has strikingly given expression to this :

"Ye instruments, forsooth, but jeer at me
With wheel and cog, and shapes uncouth of wonder;
I found the portal, you the keys should be;
Your wards are deftly wrought, but drive no bolts asunder !
Mysterious even in open day,
Nature retains her veil, despite our clamours :
That which she doth not willingly display
cannot be wrenched from her with levers, screws and hammers."[3]

3. *Faust* (Scene I, Night). Trsl. by Bayard Taylor.

But how then should it be possible to penetrate to the bottom of world ? There is but one well-defined path; it is the following one :

We, too, yea each one of us, do belong to the world; hence also our personalities ultimately have their roots in the world's *bottom*, have grown from *it*, and also we as personalities draw our strength therefrom, just as a tree has grown from the ground it stands on and draws all its strength from the latter. Therewith our own ultimate, primary bottom coincides with the bottom of the world, as much as the knowledge of the ground and soil a particular tree is rooted in also conveys us, in principle, the knowledge of the ground from which all trees upon the whole grow forth. Thus I need only return to my own bottom, I need only withdraw myself from the phenomenal world and within my personality more and more to my innermost, to my essence: as soon as I have actually penetrated thereto, and thus to the ultimate bottom on which my cognizable personality is grounded, I have at the same time penetrated to the bottom of the world, from which the entire phenomenal world again and again springs forth with all the marvels and incomprehensibilities we have previously touched on.

This right path has been followed by the ancient Āryan Indians, by the great Neo-Platonist Plotinos, and by the Christian mystics. The word "mystics", however, does not at all mean that the path itself is a mystical one, i.e. that it is shrouded in mysterious obscurity; it rather signifies that on this quite sober and reasonable path one penetrates to the solution of the mystery of one's own Self and therewith to the solution of the mystery of the world-bottom, and thus to that which is ultimately understood by the Divine. To quote but two out of many instances, the German mystic Meister Eckhart says: "Whosoever yet wishes to fathom the marvel of God easily draws his wisdom from — himself"; furthermore he states : "To the extent in which man cognises himself, to this, verily, may he come to cognise God !" And Jacob Böhme exclaims : "Where wishest thou to search for God ? In the depths beyond the stars ? Thou shalt not find him there. Search for him in thy heart, in the centre of thy vital birth; there wilt thou find him !"

Naturally, this path is not at all at our convenience, in any case not so comfortable as just strolling about on the world's surface, gazing in amazement at the wonders and horrors in which on that surface the phantasmagorias emerging from the depths of the world-bottom manifest themselves. It is indeed far more comfortable to view an imposing eruption of the Vesuvius, Etna or Cotopaxi at a distance than to descend, after the volcano has calmed down, as far as possible into the crater's interior, as some explorers have done.

Quite on the contrary, the path into the depths of our own Self not only discloses these very depths but also the primary bottom of the entire phenomenal world, wherewith it also reveals the ultimate purpose of our existence, reveals in particular, with radiant clarity, our own immortality, and reveals all the possibilities as to our future after death; finally and above all it reveals the state absolutely adequate to us and therewith the Great Peace, hence the perfect, deathless, eternal state of happiness.

B

VII

In the preceding expositions the essential contents of the religious problems have been elucidated; at the same time both the method and the path on which alone we can arrive at their solution have been disclosed. It is now the time to prove that the ancient Āryan Indians actually succeeded in solving the above-mentioned primary problems on this path.

In the very dawn of their religious development the ancient Indians, too, like all peoples, at first sought and found the world-bottom in the externally cognizable forces of nature, which they therefore personified into gods. Soon, however, they penetrated to the presentient cognition that the world's bottom cannot at all consist of a multiplicity of gods and that, on the contrary, the principle underlying the world must be an only and uniform one.

Thus already in the famous Creation Hymn of the Rigveda — "maybe the most marvellous piece of philosophy deriving from the earliest Āryan times" —it says:

> "At that time there was not non-existence, nor existence either — no atmosphere, nor any firmament beyond. — In whose shelter was the world, who then encompassed it? — Where was the profound abysm, where the sea? — There was no death then, nor was there

immortality — no night was there, nor was the day yet apparent. — Breathlessly, in primordial originality, there breathed the One beyond which no other was.— Yet who found this out — who heard whence emanates creation ? — On this side of it the gods appeared — so who then knows whence they have come ?"[4]

At this stage the answer was that at first an only, supreme personal God was enthroned, which corresponds with the common religious development of mankind; thus in the Prajāpati hymn the question of "who is the God that we shall worship with oblations ?", was answered : "Prajāpati — (that is, Lord of creatures)—, it is thou and no other who encompassest all that has come into existence." Henceforth Prajāpati became the supreme God of the Vedic pantheon.

But he, too, was only a stage of transition to the highest cognition. Also his autocracy came to an end, namely when the Āryan genius more and more found its mainstay in itself, when more and more the consciousness dawned upon it that the world-bottom, as the primary bottom of the phenomenal world, remains untouched by the ceaseless alterations of the latter (which springs forth from it), yea that the world-bottom underlies the phenomenal world, hence that it ought to be searched for in the world's very *depths*, just as, similarly, the ground on which the earth's surface rests is formed by the nickel-iron masses of the earth's very interior and these latter are in no way touched by the continuous

4. Translator's note : rendering from the German trsl. by Deussen.

changes on the earth's surface; on the very contrary, these masses first make those alterations possible. Thus one searched, as is said in the Rigveda, for "the *boneless*, that which supports all the bone-made": "Who has seen how the boneless one supports the one that first came into existence, the bone-made ?" In the Atharvaveda it is asked who the Skambha is, *the one who supports*, who bears all without himself being borne : "Make known this Skambha, who may he be ?"

It is indeed fascinating to observe how the Āryan Indian genius soon found out the very shaft leading inwards, to him who supports, to the boneless one, in short, to the world's bottom, whereby this shaft revealed itself to the Āryan Indian genius as our *own innermost*. Indeed, we can only descend into the depths within ourselves, since all external phenomena present but their outside, not their interior, their innermost, the supporting primary bottom. Thus, according to the Ushishta hymn of the Atharvaveda, all visible productions and forms of the phenomenal world rest upon the Ushishta, upon that which remains after all the externally cognizable has been stripped off. That which is left over is then called "the radiance within me". Therewith the viewpoint of the Upanishads had been arrived at, according to which our very essence, our ultimate, true Self, i.e. our Ātman — (Ātman means the Self)—is proclaimed as the ultimate, the primordial, the supporting primary bottom of ourselves.

This very essence of his, this "radiance within himself", this true Self of his must hence be searched out by him who wishes to penetrate to his primary bottom. The bare fact that we must search for this true Self of ours implies that whatever presents itself to us without our having sought it—that is, our organism with its sense-organs — cannot be our real I, our true Self, our Ātman.—

This becomes apparent without more ado : if I am deprived of my arms and legs, if I am furthermore deprived of both my nose and my eyes, I am not deprived of myself; *I myself* am still wholly intact. This true Self of mine is independent even from the vital organs, that is to say, from heart, lungs, head etc., for all these organs are also subject to constant change, so that after a period of approximately seven years no atom of my body is still the same; on the contrary, my body on the whole has by then been completely renewed. And yet, despite all parts of my body having been substituted, *I myself* am still the same, am still the very same *I* that I was and shall be throughout my life.

Thus already the ancient masters of the Upanishads found out that our body is not our true Self but a mere *attribute* — upādhi — of ourselves, just as a garment one puts on is but an attribute. But what then is our true Self ? The masters of the Upanishads answer : that which remains when the body is left out of consideration. Now what is that which remains ? Naturally our mind. This mental Self of ours can be seen, as the masters of the Upanishads say, every night in all its purity, namely when our body, in sleep, is quieted to the utmost and the outer sense-organs have become completely inactive. Being thus independent from the sleeping body our mind develops the most intense activity in our dream-life.— But even *this* activity of our mind disquiets us and thus does not afford us peace; therefore, according to the Upanishads, if we want to achieve the state absolutely adequate to us even this activity must be put an end to, so that only *completely quiescent spirituality* is left, as reigns in deep dreamless sleep. This *quiescent* spirituality is then supposed to be our real Being, our true Self, our actual Ātman, and therewith the state absolutely adequate to us.

In the Chāndogya Upanishad the whole of this Upanishadic teaching is beautifully illustrated :

> "The Self, free from sin, free from old age, free from death, free from suffering, free from hunger and thirst, this one should seek to know."

Actuated by this demand it is Indra from among the gods and Virocana of the demons who do set out on their way to Prajāpati for instruction; they stay 32 years with him as his disciples. Then Prajāpati spoke to them : "Regard your Self in a vessel full of water, and that which you do not perceive of your Self, let me know ! " Thus they looked at themselves in the vessel full of water; Prajāpati spoke to them : "What do you see ?"—They answered : "We see, Venerable One, our entire Self, down to the hairlets and nails, reflected in the water". And Prajāpati spoke to them : "Now adorn yourselves, put on your finest attire and smarten yourselves up; then again regard yourselves in the vessel full of water!" Thus they adorned themselves, put on their finest attire and smartened themselves up, and then again looked at themselves in the vessel full of water. And Prajāpati spoke to them : "What do you see ?"—They said : "Just as, Venerable

One, we stand here, adorned, in our finest attire and smartened up, just so, Venerable One, are those reflected in the water adorned, clad in their finest attire and smartened up". And Prajāpati, in order to put them to the test, spoke to them: "*This* is the Self, *this* is the immortal, the fearless".— Both disciples were satisfied with the answer; they set out for home. Prajāpati, following them with the eyes, exclaimed: "There they go, without having perceived and found the Self".

Virocana and the demons set their heart at ease with this answer; so do all demon-like men who regard their Self to be in the body, who therefore do please and coddle the latter while on earth and who deck this body up with all sorts of trash even as a corpse, as though there were any continuance of life or any world beyond for it.

Indra, however, considering that *this* Self is affected by all of the body's sufferings and infirmities and that it is annihilated with death, feels — (as indeed everybody can feel) — that whichever alteration takes place with it cannot, consequently, touch *us*; thus he returns to Prajāpati.

Prajāpati invites him to stay for 32 more years as his disciple; and Indra stays for 32 more years. Then Prajāpati gives him the second answer:

"That spirit which gaily roams about in dream, that is the Self, that is the immortal, the fearless." Yet not even this answer sets Indra's heart at ease in that he ponders: "Certainly this Self is not blind even though the body be blind, it is not lame even though the body be lame. Indeed, it is not affected by the body's infirmities; and yet it is as though they oppressed it, as though it experienced something unpleasant; in this I cannot find any consolation."

And again he returned with the firewood — i.e. as a disciple — to Prajāpati, telling him of his doubts. And Prajāpati said: "Indeed, Maghavan, so it is, that's how matters stand; but I will further elucidate the Self to you. Stay 32 more years as my disciple!" And Indra stayed for 32 more years as a disciple. Then Prajāpati spoke to him: "When one has thus dropped asleep, has come fully and completely to rest, so that one perceives no dream-vision : *that* is the Self, *that* is the immortal, the fearless."

Thereupon Indra left, his heart being set at ease. But he had not yet reached the gods when a new uncertainty assailed him. Thus he again betook himself with the firewood to Prajāpati and spoke to him: "Alas ! In this state, Venerable One, one neither knows oneself nor does one know the other beings either; in this I cannot find any consolation."— "Indeed, Maghavan, so it is, that's how matters stand", said Prajāpati, "but I will elucidate it to you still further. Stay five more years as my disciple !" And Indra stayed for five more years as a disciple. Then Prajāpati spoke to him :

"O Maghavan, mortal indeed is this body, in death's power. It is the abode of that immortal, bodiless Self. The body-bearer, however, is subject to oppression with weal and woe; for, since he bears a body, there is no warding them off. Yet he who bears no body is not touched by weal and woe."

Thus one ought to become *free from body* by submerging into the supreme light, viz. through withdrawing to pure, wholly quiescent spirituality.—

This is, according to the Upanishads, the deathless and therewith eternal state, hence the state absolutely adequate to us. This is why the Brihadāraṇyaka Upanishad says referring to it :

"Like as above in the air a falcon or an eagle after having flown about wearily folds its pinions and settles on the earth, so, too, does the mind hasten towards that state where, perfectly calmed, it feels no more desire and no longer sees any dream-visions. This is the main substance of the Self, in which it is beyond craving, free from spite and without fear.

This is the substantial form of the Self, in which all desire is quenched, Self longing but for itself; thus it is free from desire and beyond grief. Then it is not touched either by good or by evil. Then one has overcome all torments of one's heart."

Therewith has been found, according to the Upanishads, the primary bottom of our personality; it is our spiritual Self which, free from the body that alone is subject to disease, old age and death, is supposed to be immortal and, when perfectly calmed, is understood to be *wholly content in itself* and thus absolutely desireless, hence to dwell in perfect peace and therewith to all eternity in the state absolutely adequate to it.

Therewith for the Āryan Indian also the mystery of the world-bottom in the fullest sense of the word had become illuminated. For, if our own essence is pure, perfectly quiescent, immortal spirituality, the same holds true, naturally, also of everything else in the phenomenal world. The primary bottom of all this, and hence of the entire phenomenal world as a whole must be *pure, motionless spirituality.* From this ocean of pure spirituality, which is a state of absolute quiescence, the whole phenomenal world has emerged, just as the islands in the ocean emerged from its very bottom. Now the world's bottom as such is called, by the Indians, the Brahman, i.e. that which we call the impersonal Godhead. From this results the equation Ātman = Brahman. This means that in its very bottom my Self is identical with the Self of the whole world, hence with the world's bottom. Thus it is to this world-bottom that withdraws he who detaches himself from his body and thus withdraws to his own calmed spirituality.

So this is the way in which the Indians penetrated the Marvel of God: in submerging into one's own depths one finally discovered the bottom of the world, the Brahman, i.e. God. In astonishment one perceived the own unfathomable depths to be the very depths of the Godhead, that is to say, that we ourselves ultimately are this Godhead. Thus an Upanishad makes known: "Brahman he is and into Brahman he submerges", words hence expressing the self-same as these others: "Worshipping the Self with this offering, he submerges into his Self's own splendour."

This way of arriving at the solution of the primary problem has been followed also by the religious geniuses of the Occident, such as Plotinos and the Christian mystics; and they did follow it with the like result. Just a few thoughts of the German mystic Meister Eckhart shall be quoted here:

"Where I am, there is God; this is the naked truth" —

"Man is in truth God and God is in truth man"—

"In this transcending I experience God and I to be one"— and finally:

"Verily, wilt thou find the noble birth thou must return to the origin and the bottom from which thou hast come."

C

VIII

However evident it is that this is the exact method for penetrating *cognitively* the primary problem, and however evident it is that thereby the problem of the Self and that of God ultimately merge into each other—(i.e. that the primary bottom of our own Self or, to express it in Occidental terms, of our soul, coincides with the primary bottom of the whole world, i.e. with God)—, so did none the less, as shall be seen afterwards, neither the ancient masters of the Indian Vedas, nor the great Greek philosophers, not even their culmination, the Neo-Platonist Plotinos, yea not even the Christian mystics nor Meister Eckhart either actually penetrate to the ultimate depths of our own Being and hence to the world's *real* primary bottom. Only *one* man succeeded in elucidating our own real primary bottom and hence the actual primary bottom of the whole world. This one man, — like most religious geniuses an Āryan — was Siddhatta Gotama, an Indian king's son, called, on account of his unique discovery, the Buddha, i.e. "He who has awakened to the Supreme Reality". He is also named the Sage from the clan of the Sakyans and lived from about 560 to 480 B.C. He was thirty years of age when he forsook the luxury of Indian nobility in order to go forth into homelessness as a mendicant with the aim of making himself *absolutely free from suffering*.

Now all suffering, especially the suffering of disease and death, is conditioned by our body, which may be called a regular machine of suffering. On this account Lao Tse asks: "What could ever torment him who has no body?" So one can become free from suffering solely if it is possible to make oneself *free from any body*. This, however, presupposes the body not pertaining *essentially* to us, i.e. that it is not unseverably bound up with our Self. As stated above, already the Vedic seers and the greatest among the Occidental religious geniuses had both become conscious of the correctness of this presupposition and taught it. Also Gotama, the Buddha, soon attained to the cognition of this truth; yea, he not only taught the very fact of our corporeality not being essential to us, but he also cogently demonstrated it, which we shall see later on. Precisely thereby he arrived at the heights of the other religious geniuses who stated that our true Being must consist in pure spirituality, free from corporeality. Yet at this very point the Buddha's first great discovery manifests itself: the Buddha showed that it is impossible for there to be pure spirituality free from any corporeality, i.e. a wholly incorporeal spirit, that, on the very contrary, whatever kind of spirituality is always and without exception bound to a corporeal form. This, however, even by itself involved enormous consequences: thereby the final result of the whole Vedic and Greek wisdom, yea of the whole wisdom of all mystics—according to which the essence of man is supposed to consist precisely in pure, incorporeal spirituality—was overturned; at the same time the proclamation of this pure spirituality as the state absolutely adequate to us proved to be an illusion. For, since every corporeal form is subject to death, any spirituality must consequently come to an end together with the corporeal form it is essentially bound to. Thus there is as little an immortal spirit as there is an immortal body. Hence it follows that even pure spirituality cannot be the state absolutely adequate to us, cannot bring us absolute happiness, *precisely because it, too, is bound to die.*

Does not this part of the Buddha's Teaching, if it is really true, reduce to naught all that which we have hitherto come to know as the very culmination of human wisdom? On this very account it is of the greatest importance to know the argument the Buddha advances on this part of his Teaching. This argument is, in short, the following: Our essence is supposed to be spiritual. Now what do we understand by the word "spiritual"? Spirit or mind is equivalent to consciousness. This consciousness itself is a visual consciousness, an auditive, olfactory, gustatory, tactile and mental consciousness. According to its intensity it divides into sensation, perception and thinking: at first one has a sensation of something, then that which has been felt is perceived and thereupon it is thought over. Thus it is these different manifestations of consciousness what we summarise in the word "spirit". Now let us consider: if we lose our eyes we shall no longer have any visual sensation and perception, in short, any visual consciousness; if we become deaf we shall have no more auditive sensation and therewith no auditive consciousness either; if our nose and our tongue are out of function we shall have no more olfactory and gustatory sensations and hence no such consciousness; in so far as our body as organ of touch loses its sensitivity — (e.g. when anaesthetised)— also the tactile consciousness ceases; even thinking shall be put an end to if the organ of thought is seriously hurt, in which case there would be no more consciousness at all. Thus all feeling, all perceiving and thinking and hence all consciousness or spirituality upon the whole depend on our body's material sense-organs including the organ of thought and are conditioned by them; thus all mental functions are *organic* functions, i.e. functions of our corporeal organism. Hence it follows that it is as impossible for there to be a mental activity without material sense-organs, in particular without an organ of thought, as for there to be a digestion without a digestive organ. Consequently, all consciousness and hence all spirituality depend on our corporeal life.

Hence, consciousness or man's mind proves to be a light tied to and dependent on our body, where it flares up ever and ever anew, just as the light of a candle is tied to and dependent on the latter, on which it flares up ever and ever again.[5]

This is the reason why the light of consciousness or mind necessarily must perish with the dissolution of our body in death, just as the light of a candle perishes along with the combustion and hence

5. In Samyutta-Nikāya xxii, 136, it is said : "The body, ye bhikkhus, is glowing ash". The glow is consciousness.— In Dīgha-Nikāya, Sutta No. 2,83, a bhikkhu, inspired by the Buddha, says: "This body of mine is shaped, has arisen from the four main elements, has been generated by father and mother, is but a heap of rice-pap and sour gruel, is impermanent, doomed to destruction, dissolution, decay and annihilation, and this is *my consciousness, tied to and dependent on it.*"

destruction of the latter.

These are the reasons why according to the Buddha after the body's dissolution there is no more consciousness, no independent spirituality or mind.

But does this interpretation not imply the crassest materialism? Certainly not; the Buddha thereby merely takes into account the well-founded objection on the part of materialism, namely that there cannot at all be a spirituality or mind without a body. On the other hand, however, it was precisely this knowledge that served the Buddha actually to penetrate to the ultimate depths of our Self or soul, namely thus: The Buddha sought to find out our *true* Self, i.e. that which is our very Being, hence that through the annihilation of which we ourselves should be totally annihilated. Whenever the question is finding out a particular object, at least *one* unmistakable characteristic of the latter must be known. So if I go in search of gold I must know at least *one* specific characteristic of it lest I should run the risk of taking copper, brass or yellow mica for the gold I am searching for. Likewise I must previously know at least *one* unmistakable characteristic of my true Self, of that in which I ultimately consist, if I want to exclude the risk of taking for my Self something that in reality is *not* my Self, be it that this something in question has nothing at all to do with my Self, or that it is but a non-essential attribute of mine.

The unmistakable charateristic as to the knowledge of the very reality of my true Self is declared by the Buddha to be the following:

"That which I see arise and pass away, and due

to its transitoriness cause me suffering, cannot be I myself."

If the cash-box in which I keep my money has been stolen, undoubtedly nothing pertaining to my Self has been thereby taken away; for, even long after the loss of the cash-box took place it causes me sorrow, and it is I myself who perceives this loss. Let us now regard our body as concerns this characteristic of our Self : our body consists throughout of the material elements of the external world, namely, as the Buddha states, of earth, water, fire and air. Now for these materials to build up our body they must be converted into specific, vitally important chemical combinations in order to be *assimilated* by the body. This takes place through *nutrition*; the latter must be, however, a regular one since the material assimilated by the body is soon used up, i.e. broken down into waste substances, hence *disassimilated*, and thereupon excreted. This results in a constant *metabolism* throughout the body. None of the latter's cells is excepted therefrom. In particular the cells of the nerves and of the myocardium are subject to it; also their life consists in an uninterrupted assimilation and disassimilation of the material that builds them up, all this taking place through nutrition and constant excretion. As a consequence thereof, after a certain lapse of time (usually estimated at seven years) each one of the cells of our body has become a different one as to the matter building it up. Hence it follows that we are furnished with a completely new body every seven years. If I am, for instance, 35 years of age at present, I have, in reality, already changed my body five times by now. Yet I myself have always been and remained the same; it is only my body that becomes a different one, which I can constantly observe. Moreover, I regret this constant alteration of my body in the very moment it takes a turn for the worse. As an aged man, for instance, I bemoan not being any longer in the possession of the vigorous body I had as a youth or a man. Therewith I deplore something *that has long ago ceased to exist*. Now that which I still bemoan after it has already ceased to exist, namely the body I had possessed as a youth and that which I had possessed as a man, can by no means have been I myself!

Had it been I who then ceased to exist I certainly could not be lamenting now. Now if the loss of the body I had as a child, and of the body I had as a youth, and of the further body I possessed as a man has not taken *me* along with it, then certainly the loss of the body I shall have as an aged man won't take me along with it either. Thus the body evidently is not my Self.

As stated above, our mental functions depend on the material sense-organs of our body, including the organ of thought. Hence a further consequence follows, namely that also these mental functions together with consciousness do not pertain inseparably to my Self: "How could it be possible for the mind to be the Self, since it arises in dependence upon that which is not the Self?", asks the Buddha.

If a piano is not my own, the sounds I call forth by its means are all the less my property. According to the Buddha our body, too, is a kind of piano on which we play. The keys are the sense-organs together with the organ of thought, and that which we call forth or produce are the sensations, perceptions and thoughts and therewith consciousness on the whole. Thus our body is but the *apparatus* by means of which we do *produce* all that, it is, hence, only the *apparatus* for the production of cognition, hence the cognizing-apparatus. By reason of this all mental functions and thus all consciousness may just as well perish together with our body; we ourselves shall thereby not at all be touched in our substantiality: the end of our *body* and of the consciousness dependent on it shall not be *our* end.

Thus we are merely *entangled* in our body, on which that which we call mind grows like a parasite, the rope causing this entanglement being our *thirst*, our craving for a body and a mind.[6] The result of this entanglement is our very *defilement:* "Since body and mind[7] do bring also weal and not only suffering, the beings do crave for body and mind; it is by reason of this craving that the beings bind themselves up with them, and in consequence of this attachment they become defiled", the Buddha says to Mahāli the Licchavi.[8] Elsewhere body and mind are called *garments* we ourselves are clad with and which the Delivered One strips off: "I have put off all garments; there is no further Becoming for me", triumphantly

6. This thirst after a body not only actuates us in our death, on letting go our present body, to grasp a new germ from which a new organism shall develop (see below !), but this thirst after life is at the same time the primary force that keeps the body in action throughout life, in particular also the body's metabolism.

7. The Buddha always speaks of the "five groups of grasping", viz. corporeal form, sensation, perception, mental activities and cognition.

8. Samyutta-Nikāya xxii, 60.— Compare this with the following sentence of the Vedānta : "The absolutely pure one enters the absolutely impure body" (Deussen, *Das System des Vedānta*, p. 274).

exclaims Vītaśoka in the Psalms of the Monks. Yea, in the 75th Sutta of Majjhima-Nikāya the Buddha compares our being in love with our body and mind to a blind-born man taking a pride in the grimy coarse robe he wears and which somebody has passed off upon him for a fine, white garment. Furthermore, the Buddha characterises body and mind as *toys* we do play with as boys and girls do with sand-castles: "As long as these boys and girls are not free from craving, free from desire, from attachment and thirst with regard to these sand-castles, so long are they attached to them, do they enjoy them, are concerned about them, regard them as their own. As soon, however, as they have become free from craving, free from desire, from attachment and thirst as to these sand-castles, they pull them down with their hands and feet, destroy them, and do no longer play with them: likewise, Rādha, thou do pull down both body and mind, do destroy them, annihilate them, desist from playing with them, do devote thyself to the annihilation of the thirst after them!"[9] This exhortation of the Master was put into practice to such an extent by Sāriputta, the greatest disciple of the Buddha, that he could tell the latter: "Like as if a man, Lord, were to carry about a pot filled with fat and dripping from many holes, so do I carry about this body dripping from many holes."

IX

But what are we, since we are neither body nor mind? *Everything* in the phenomenal world is composed of

9. Samyutta-Nikāya xiii, 2.

body and mind, yea the former consists *solely* of these two elements, albeit in quite different degrees and combinations. Something being neither body nor mind is, since beyond the phenomenal world, not to be grasped with cognition, just as the ultra-violet rays cannot be perceived with the eyes; this is why we cannot even imagine it. Therewith it is, for us, inconceivable, uncharacterizable, unfathomable.

Thus our true Self, just because it is beyond our body and our mind, is unimaginable, uncognizable, uncharacterizable, unfathomable: "An Accomplished One, freed from body and mind, is profound, immeasurable, unfathomable like the great Ocean", declares the Buddha[10]; and Meister Eckhart says: "The soul has — (after its Deliverance) —lost its name in the unity of the Divine Being; therefore it is there no longer named soul; its name is 'immeasurable Being'". Furthermore he states: "What the soul is in its ultimate bottom, this has not yet been found."

But why is our true Self not to be made out through cognition? For what reason can be only cognised that which is *not* our Self? Because all cognition is turned outwards. It is just as when a motorist drives along a road by night. He sees whatever enters the range of the dazzling light of his car's headlamps as clear as by day; he himself, however, does not enter the light's range because he is placed behind it, for which reason he is not able to see himself in the darkness. On account of this it says in the Upanishads: "Outwards pierced the openings the Being-in-itself—(our true Self)—;

10. Samyutta-Nikāya xliv, 1.

therefore one sees outwards, but not into the Inner Self." As far as this also Schopenhauer has seen to the bottom; he says: "The eye is the dark point in consciousness, just as on the retina the precise point of entry of the optic nerve is blind, the brain itself is wholly insensible, the body of the sun itself is dark, and the eye sees everything except itself. Our faculty of cognition is directed entirely outwards. Therefore every one knows of himself only as of this individual. If, on the other hand, he could bring to consciousness what he is besides and beyond this, he would willingly give up his individuality and smile at the tenacity of his attachment to this."[11]

If, however, our true Self is beyond the phenomenal world, it is at the same time beyond impermanence, for impermanence and phenomenal world are the selfsame thing: "In the order of the Sublime One that which is impermanent is called the world", says the Buddha.[12] Therewith our true Self is also beyond all that which is sorrow-bringing, for only that which is impermanent brings suffering.

Thus it is evident that he who has rooted out any thirst for the impermanent and in particular for his own body and mind, and who has thereby become *absolutely* will-less, desireless, free from thirst — (we can crave only for the impermanent as something alien to us which we do not already possess)—, and who in this absolute desirelessness with regard to all that which is alien to him has withdrawn into himself, indeed, *in him dwells, precisely in consequence*

11. "World as Will and Representation", vol. II, ch.41. (Trsl. by E.F.J. Payne.)

12. Samyutta-Nikāya xxxv, 84.

of this absolute desirelessness, the highest self-contentment and thus *boundless inward Peace,* therewith the state *absolutely adequate* and thus *perfect* well-being.

Thus we need only for ever detach ourselves in perfect desirelessness from our body and our mind, and withdraw *into ourselves*, into our *true* Self as our primary bottom which is free from any *attributes*, hence into *Nibbana*—and we shall thereby come into possession of the deathless, eternal, perfect well-being (acalam sukham).[13] This bliss has been also taken into possession by the Buddha with his withdrawal into himself: "I now leave ye alone and go away—I have chosen *the refuge in myself*",[14] he said to his bhikkhus on the approach of his death.[15] With this withdrawal to ourselves, to our transcendent, deathless Essence, according to the Buddha the following words will apply also to us: "What do you think, Mahārāja, have you a calculator or a mintmaster who might be able to measure the water of the great ocean, so that he might say: 'So many quarts

---

13. The ultimate religious goal of Buddhism is commonly called the *Nibbāna* (Nirvāna). This word means "extinction", namely extinction of all craving ("thirst") for that which is alien. In the "Psalms of the Monks" (No. 691) as well as elsewhere this word is traced back to nis+vana, 'nis' being equivalent to our suffix 'less', while 'vana' means=desire. Hence also thereafter Nibbāna=desirelessness (with regard to body, mind and all that which they convey): "After having driven out thirst one speaks of Nibbāna (Samyutta-Nikāya i, ch. 7,4).—"The extirpation of the greedy desire for body and mind : this is the annihilation of suffering" (Majjhima-Nikāya, 28th Sutta).

14. Dīgha-Nikāya, 16th Sutta.

15. Compare this with Samyutta-Nikāya xxii, 95, where it says : "Let the bhikkhu give up any *entanglement* (in the components of his personality —kandhe—) and let him take refuge *in himself.*"—With regard to the "entanglement" see above, p. 36.

of water, or so many hundreds, or so many thousands, or so many hundreds of thousands of quarts of water are therein'?—'Such a man I have not, Reverend One, since the great ocean is indeed profound, immeasurable, unfathomable.'—'It is just the same, Mahārāja, as if one wished to comprehend an Accomplished One by the predicates of body and mind. In an Accomplished One body and mind are done away with, uprooted throughout, so that they cannot at all develop anew. An Accomplished One, Mahārāja, freed from body and mind, is profound, immeasurable, unfathomable like the great ocean."[16]

This primary bottom of ours, and therewith also the bottom of the world, stands for the *absolute* reality that Schopenhauer has in view in the following words: "When we wake up from a dream that vividly affects us, what convinces us of its nothingness is not so much its disappearance as the emergence of a second reality which lay concealed under the reality (of the dream) so powerfully affecting us, and which now comes to the fore. We all really have a permanent notion or presentiment that, under this reality in which we live and are, there also lies concealed a second and different reality : it is the thing-in-itself, the *hypar* (the real in the proper sense) to this *onar* (our present life-dream)."[17] It is to this *absolute* reality that the Buddha has awakened; this

16. Samy.-Nik. xliv, 1. — We see that here, as also elsewhere, the Self that has succeeded in detaching itself from its "attributes", i.e. from body and mind or, as it says in the 51st Sutta of Majjh.-Nikāya, the "holy become Self" — hence that which we call the true Self —is named "an Accomplished One" in contradistinction to the undelivered Self of the other beings.

17. "Handschriftl. Nachlass", p. 342. Trsl. by E.F.J. Payne.

is why he called himself "one who has awakened from dream" (suttappabuddho).

This absolute reality, "the very point of rest of the universe",[18] is our eternal destination. It is in this reality, which at the same time is "the very mainstay of the universe"[19] that also roots the marvel of human and any other organism with all their mental powers, artistic impulses and urge for beauty. There the marvels of the plant and mineral world have their roots. There, in this very reality, also root all the countless worlds presenting themselves to us as the starry sky along with their unalterable laws. In it has its roots everything upon the whole; "In thy Naught—(the primary bottom can by no means be penetrated to by cognition)—I hope to find the All": there it is realised. But this All roots there in its uncharacterizable, unconceivable primary state: "There earth, water, fire and air have no access to;[20] there do not—(for this reason)—light any stars, nor beams the sun nor doth the moon shine forth; *yet no darkness either doth there dwell"*, says the Buddha.[21] All what is positive, all what is conceivable, in particular also all that which is good as well as evil, has first come into existence on this side of the phenomenal world.

For him who has found his way back to his primary bottom and therewith to the grandeur of Nibbāna there remains, as "the most sublime of

18. Kaivalya-Upanishad 16.
19. Mahānār.-Upan. ii, 7.
20. Compare with the words of Meister Eckhart : "In itself the soul is without matter, like as God."
21. Udāna i, 10.

whatever there is among the produced and not-produced", *"the Great Peace"* — *"eternal stillness"*.

This very uncharacterizableness and grandeur of our primary bottom has also been divined by Meister Eckhart, in that he says with Dionysius Areopagite: "The primordial thing is beyond all name, it withdraws from love, comprehension and grasping, it is above 'Being', above 'nature', it is *neither light nor darkness.* Verily, how utterly alien is this bottom to all what rests on a ground!"—"There dwells",—"in inscrutable stillness"—"in a stillness imperceptibly fading away",—"only profound silence".—"Whosoever has looked into this bottom, be it but for an instant, to him, indeed, thousand thalers of red beaten gold are but a false farthing."

The wise Yājñavalkya, who likewise followed the tracks of the Buddha's Teaching—(remember the above-quoted words of the Buddha: "I have chosen *the refuge in myself*")—, gives expression to this state of affairs as follows :

> "If only man fathomed the I
> And knew who he was *in truth*,
> How could he ever crave for the body?
> With what desire, which purpose for?"

This very goal is claimed by another Upanishad to be that of the Delivered One; it says there: "Whether he quits the body in a sacred place or in a dog-flesh eater's hovel, he merges into the Absolute; he shakes off the breath of life and merges into the Absolute."

Consequently, he who wishes to take into possession the perfect, eternal well-being[22] must return thither, i.e. to himself beyond his personality, hence to the Absolute or, as says the Buddha, to the "absolute state" (padam asankhatam) as the "beyond of the sphere of perception".[23]

22. As follows from the previous expositions (cp. VII), the difference between the Vedānta and also Meister Eckhart on the one hand and the Buddha on the other lies in the former stating that the Absolute is already achieved with pure spirituality, whereas according to the Buddha it presupposes even the overcoming of mind or spirit.

23. Majjhima-Nikāya, 7th Sutta.

D

X

Naturally, this is easier said than done; it supposes the very demand of detaching ourselves for ever from our body and our mind and thereby for ever renouncing our personality or, in brief, altogether disappearing from the phenomenal world. Indeed, who is actually able to do so? Maybe every five hundred years one of the four thousand millions of men that populate the earth. What then does, according to the Buddha, await these others after death?

As we have seen our body is, as stated by the Buddha, a mere *attribute* of ours. Thus we have already been before our body developed. Hence the following question arises: how then have we come to this body? The reply most probably will be: "Why, naturally through procreation on the part of my father and my mother." Here, however, the following objection could be raised: "Now this germ prepared by my father and my mother, what did it concern me who have existed previously and independently of it? Certainly not more than any other germ that has been prepared elsewhere." Hence it is evident that I myself as *the third one* must have somehow participated in the act of my procreation, in consequence of which participation the germ prepared by my father and my mother then became *my* germ and furthermore *my* body. Now when does something become mine? When, for instance, does the apple on a tree become *my* apple? Undoubtedly when I make it my own, when I *grasp* it. And when do I make it my own, when do I grasp it? When I have a desire for it, i.e. when I *will* it. Had I no desire for it I should never think of grasping it, and should I not grasp it, it certainly would not come to be my own, i.e. it would not become *my* apple. In quite the same way the germ prepared by my parents naturally could only have become *my* germ through my having grasped and clung to it, in consequence of which that germ, when it developed into a corporeal organism, became *my* corporeal organism. And I did grasp that germ, I did cling to it, because I had the desire, the will thus to build up a corporeal organism for me. Hence it was my *will* for a body that actuated me to construct in my mother's womb a body by appropriating the germ prepared by my father and mother, just as at present it is my will to use this body uninterruptedly for producing sensations and perceptions of the world.[24]

Now where did that will of ours for a body come from before our conception? We need the body in

---

24. How are we to represent to ourselves that grasping of a germ, a grasping that has its roots in the Unfathomable? It is as impossible to represent this to oneself as it is to represent to oneself one's will. Or is there anybody who has already seen his will? And yet it is possible to comprehend that grasping, namely by comparing it to the magnetic attraction or to the power of attraction that makes the sun maintain its planets in its orbit. Also with regard to these drawing forces which, defined in Buddhist terms, likewise are acts of grasping that emanate from the Unfathomable, solely their very reality can be stated, but not the nature of their activity.

order to be capable of seeing forms, of hearing sounds, smelling odours, tasting flavours, touching tangible objects and thinking thoughts or, what is the same thing, in order to experience, by means of it, sensations and perceptions of the world's objects; for, our body actually is the very apparatus for producing sensations and perceptions or, briefly, the cognizing-*apparatus:* without the body together with its sense-organs we cannot at all see, hear, smell, taste, touch and think, and consequently we can neither feel nor perceive, just as one cannot call forth musical sounds without a musical instrument. This is the only purpose for which we want to possess our body : he who actually does not want to see anything more certainly will not care when all those parts of his body perish that make it possible for there to be a visual activity; likewise, he who has no more desire to hear, to smell, to taste and to touch anything any longer shall cling to his body merely in so far as it represents the instrument necessary for thinking, which alone is still considered to be indispensable. He who in addition to this grows weary of all thinking has actually lost any concern in his body's further existence, since it has then become superfluous. Hence it is clear that for us the body is merely a means to an end, namely to make it possible for us to experience and perceive the phenomena of the world through it. Consequently, if previous to our conception we had a longing, a will for a body and on account of this clung to the germ prepared by our parents and from which henceforth developed our body, then that very will, that longing in us was a will, a craving for experiencing and perceiving in this wise the phenomena of the world. Hence it follows that at bottom our only concern was the enjoyment of these phenomena, i.e., we wanted to come into contact with them through the agency of the body as the six-senses-machine. Now before I assumed my present body I certainly could have had a desire, a longing for these phenomena of the world only if I had already experienced and perceived and hence enjoyed them before. What the eye does not see the heart does not long for or, in other words: that which I do not know I cannot crave for. From this it follows that I must have seen, heard, smelt, tasted and touched the phenomena of the world already before the development of my present body. Now this could have come about only through the agency of the sense-organs of a corporeal organism, just as also at present I can experience the world only by means of such organs of sense. Consequently, previous to my present corporeal organism I must have had another one, by means of which I was in contact with the world. Thus I actually had, before my present body, another body with which at that time I dwelt in the world experiencing and perceiving it. So it was already then that I came to love the world, and therefrom ensued that very will which determined me, at the dissolution of my former body, to cling to the germ prepared by my parents in order thus to build up a new body for me and to enjoy the world afresh by means of its sense-organs.

But how did I come to that body previous to my present one ? Naturally in the same way in which I came to the latter : the longing, the will for such a body had also driven me to it, a will that had arisen in me in consequence of my use of a still earlier body, and so back into the beginningless past.—Yet all this holds likewise good of the immeasurable future : also in my coming death I shall cling to a new germ in a new maternal womb if I still desire to keep in contact with the world through a corporeal organism. And for the very same reason, after the dissolution of that future body of mine I shall build up in a similar way a new body for me, and after that one a new one again and so forth in *saecula saeculorum*, as long as I do not withdraw myself into my primary bottom, into my true Self that is free from any attributes, and therewith to the Absolute Reality—*the circle of our rebirths turns round.*

This doctrine of rebirth as taught by the Buddha is a cogent consequence of the very knowledge made transparently clear by him that our body is not our true Self but a mere attribute of ours, hence that it is, at bottom, something alien to us; it is also a consequence of the further knowledge that we can only assume something alien to us by grasping it, by grasping it ever and ever anew, as long as we still *want* such an attribute, as we *crave* for it: because I myself am not touched by the arising and passing away of my corporeality, I have already been previous to it, yea I actually have been at every moment before it, since then no change and thus no time could have affected *me*. Consequently, I shall also be throughout the time to come. In fact, I was and I shall be just as I *want* to be, that is to say endowed with a corporeal organism, as long as I want to possess one. Indeed, we hitherto wanted to possess such an organism, which our own will demonstrates us if only we observe it : even at present this attachment to our body is quite active in us, and as long as it is so we need not concern about the possession of such a body : the will for life is sure of its realization. Thus the beginninglessness and (possible) endlessness of our rebirths become the mirror of our own Being and, accordingly, "the world's infinity becomes the measure of our own immeasurableness that always surpasses it".[25]

Because the doctrine of rebirth is a primary truth it existed at all times and exists even nowadays in India; it was already taught in Greece about the time of the Buddha by Orphism, then by the Pythagoreans, by Empedocles, Socrates, Plato and Plotinos; likewise did and do adhere to it many great thinkers of our time. In particular it was also Goethe who, after his intellect had for a long time opposed to it, accepted the doctrine of reincarnation and remained true to it to his death: "Long have I been opposed to it, but finally I yielded: when the old man turns to dust the new one doth awaken. As long as thou graspest not this die! — become ! thou art but a gloomy guest on this sombre earth."

Now what can we be reborn as after our death? Were we *essentially* human beings we naturally could only be reborn as such, for one cannot change one's essential nature. But since our present human body at bottom is as alien to us as any other body, we can grasp in our death just as well a non-human germ, that is to say also a germ in an animal womb or in a hell-world, or in a world of light

25. The necessity for the rebirth of beings also follows from their eternal destination (cp. above, p. 6), in that this destination, namely the absolutely adequate state, cannot at all be realised in but *one* existence.

which we use to call heaven : *because we ourselves are nothing of the world, we can become everything in it.* The fact that we can become in particular also an animal has been emphasized also by Socrates, Plato and Plotinos, who likewise were great geniuses. Let us refer in particular to Plato's Phaedo, by the reading of which we shall at the same time be edified by Socrates' most sublime death.

Now what kind of a germ shall we cling to in our death according to the Buddha ? That depends, the latter says, on the nature of our will, though of course not only on our conscious will but on our will down to its deepest roots; that is to say, it depends on our innermost character as this becomes evident when it manifests itself as thirst, as blind impulse. It is precisely in this very condition that our will shall be in the decisive moment of death, when it is compelled to leave hold of the body it had hitherto clung to, and to seize a new germ. Together with the stopping of all sense-activities then also ceases all consciousness, so that, untouched by death, our thirst for a new body operates wholly disregarding the ensuing consequences, since it is no longer illuminated by any cognition and is, hence, totally blind: it necessarily leads to the grasping of the very germ that most corresponds to it, i.e. the germ that has an *elective affinity* to it. Quite equally, lightning strikes and kindles only an object that has an elective affinity for it, i.e. a wet one.[26] Accordingly does the thirst lead to the grasping of an animal germ when its nature is an animal one, to the

26. This law of elective affinity determining the kind of rebirth is set forth also by Socrates in Plato's Phaedo.

grasping of a human germ when a dying being's thirsting will is specifically human, and it leads to an attachment in a world of light when the thirsting will of the dying being has attained to the moral height of a suprahuman, divine world. If, however, the thirsting will is degenerate to such an extent that it not even has any elective affinity to the animal world, then it leads to an attachment in a yet lower world, namely in the abysses, where the beings rejected by all the other realms of life are gathered. Only later on, when the new-grasped germ has developed and when along with the setting-in of sense-activity again dawns consciousness, that which one has grasped and clung to is thrown light on by the latter, so that one then finds oneself to be an animal, a human being, a god or a devil.—This is, according to the Indian point of view and in particular after the Buddha, how the possibilities of rebirth present themselves.

As concerns in particular the heavenly worlds, which the Indian Āryans at all times called the worlds of gods, they are those realms of existence lying between the human realm and the definitive return into the primary bottom, and which the Buddha hence declares to have passed through on his return into this primary bottom, just as he declares also to have seen, in deepest concentration of the mind, the very abysses of existence.

The extent to which in particular the higher realms of existence we can emigrate to actually are a postulate of reason follows from the fact that even a mind as critical as Kant attributes them a degree of credibility that is not far from certainty; in order to characterise the relationship of the inhabitants of those higher realms of existence to us Kant quotes the following words of Pope: "Those higher beings regard our Newton just as we do regard an ape."[27] And Goethe exclaims: "Let man be noble, helpful and good — for this alone distinguishes him from all the beings we know. — Hail to *the unknown higher beings* whom we *divine* ! — Let man be like them, and may his example make us believe them !"

This is, in pithy outlines, the cognitive solution of the fundamental religious problems as found by the Indian genius. In any case it has thereby at the same time become evident that all deeper religious cognition on the whole moves along this course and runs into it.

27. Kant, "Allg. Naturgeschichte und Theorie des Himmels : Von den Bewohnern der Gestirne".

E

XI

Let us once more survey the whole: all beings, in particular also the human beings, find themselves in a wholly inadequate state. In reality they are as distant from a state *absolutely* adequate to them as heaven is from earth. But it is precisely such a suitable state that every being longs for as the highest happiness: the thirsting will for an *absolutely* adequate state is the *primary impulse* of whatever lives. Now the fulfilment of the *primary impulse* common to *all beings* must at all events be possible. Indeed, nature infallibly achieves the purposes it strives after in the beings' impulsive forces, albeit ultimately only after biological lapses of time: though nature is not omnipotent, it is all-capable. Hence it is a matter of fact that the beings must be endowed with the capability to satisfy their deepest, yea at bottom sole, *primary impulse*.

Now this capability, how is it to be developed, how is it to be realised, *how* is the primary impulse to be quenched? This is the great *primary problem*, a problem as great as its object, the primary impulse.

The attempt to arrive at a solution of this primary problem implies one indisputable fact: within the part of reality to which we are confined, or rather banished it is altogether impossible for there to be a state *absolutely* adequate to us, since there rules death, the fact that the beings are doomed to die, and therewith the very opposite from a state absolutely adequate to us. Thus the primary problem proves to be a *religious* problem, since the purpose of religion is precisely to reveal that part of reality in which the laws ruling over the realm of reality we are at present placed in have no validity or, as the Buddha says, to reveal that part of reality "to which earth, water, fire and air —(to which all natural laws apply) — have no access."

The religions themselves divide into religions of belief and cognitive or philosophical religions. Among the latter are the religion of a Socrates, of a Plato and a Plotinos, then that of the Occidental mystics who likewise have elaborated their religious attitude through own cognition. In particular the great India religions of the Vedas and of the Buddha count among the philosophical religions.

The results these philosophical religions arrived at in their attempt to find a solution of the primary problem have been briefly educidated in the foregoing expositions. They may be summarised as follows: the absolutely adequate state has been attained when we do not lack anything, i.e. when we do not at all miss anything any longer. This state we commonly seek to approach by trying to get the missing goods. This, however, is quite impossible, for the simple reason that everything without exception is doomed to impermanence, wherewith it is taken away from us over and over again. Accordingly, this way of striving after the absolutely adequate state proves to be a *sisyphean labour*, and to acquiesce in it we can but assume the "heroic attitude towards life" proclaimed by Schopenhauer. The very fact that this way is a wrong one follows from the previous statement that the achievement of the absolutely adequate state *must* be possible.—The solution of the primary problem as found by the philosophical religions, however, is astonishingly simple: it is a *grotesque delusion* that we lack something; we actually do not lack anything at all. It is solely by reason of this enormous *delusion* that from time immemorial the will, the craving, the thirst to attribute something to us grows from within ourselves, namely the thirst to attribute to us as much as possible, in particular a body and a mind. Thus we need only dissolve this delusion by seeing through it, and we shall not only not grasp anything more, but we then actually shall not be able to grasp anything more. For, in the same measure we do renounce, we approach the absolutely adequate state, yea we ourselves experience it in the boundless peace that takes possession of us and therewith in overflowing well-being, beginning with the heavenly states which are reached with the giving-up of all *earthly* up to the very summit of absolute desirelessness with regard to *every* body and mind: "God is eternal rest, for he doth not seek or will anything—*if thou wilt nothing either, thou art as much as He.*"[28] To him who strives after attaining the *absolute* well-being and therewith after the *absolutely* adequate state, the philosophical religions do not call, as categorical imperative for his conduct, "grasp!", but "give up!"—*This is the sages' stone.*

28. Angelus Silesius.

BIBLIOGRAPHY

List of works by George Grimm

The Doctrine of the Buddha. The Religion of Reason and Meditation. 3rd enlarged edition. 413 pages. Motilal Banarsidass, Delhi, 1973.

Buddhist Wisdom. The Mystery of the Self. 2nd. revised and enlarged edition. 70 pages. Motilal Banarsidass, Delhi, 1978.

Die Lehre des Buddho. Die Religion der Vernunft und der Meditation. 516 pp.-16th ed. in 1957. Reprinted in 1976 & 1979 with 16,000 copies at Lowit-Verlag, Wiesbaden/Fed. Rep. Germany.

Der Samsāro. Die Weltenirrfahrt der Wesen. 2nd revised edition, 128 pages. H. Schwab-Verlag, Schopfheim/Fed. Rep. Germany, 1960.

Der Buddhaweg für Dich. 2nd edition, 248 pages. E. Skrleta-Verlag, Vienna/Austria, 1974.

Die Botschaft des Buddha, der Schluessel zur Unsterblichkeit. 2nd edition, 86 pages. E. Skrleta-Verlag, Vienna/Austria, 1975.

Ewige Fragen. Die Religiosen Grundprobleme und ihre Losung im Indischen Geiste. 4th edition, 83 pages. E. Skrleta-Verlag, Vienna, 1975.

Buddhistische Meditationen. A breviary. 2nd enlarged edition, 396 pages. H. Bauer KG und Baum-Verlag, Freiburg/Fed. Rep. Germany, 1962.

Buddhistische Weisheit. Das Geheimnis des Ich. 4th enlarged edition. 128 pages. H. Schwab-Verlag, Schopfheim/Fed. Rep. Germany, 1961.

Das Glück, die Botschaft des Buddho. 4th enlarged edition, 160 pages. H. Bauer KG und Baum-Verlag, Freiburg/Fed. Rep. Germany, 1960.

Die Wissenschaft des Buddhismus. 2nd revised edition. 431 pages. Altbuddhistische Gemeinde, Utting/ Fed. Rep. Germany, 1978.

La Religion du Bouddha. La Religion de la Connaisance. 2nd edition, 306 pages. Adrien Maisonneuve, Paris. 1944.

La Sagesse du Bouddha. Le Mystere du Moi. 2nd French edition, 1931. Librairie Orientaliste P. Geuthner, Paris.

Tuê-Giác Cũa Phât. 1st Vietnamese edition. Saigon, 1964.

GENERAL INDEX

INDEX OF PROPER NAMES